THE LAST OF A DYING BREED

My maternal grandfather was a remarkable man ...

The world knew him as **Glen EagleSpeaker**, a renowned multi-media artist, who created countless massive murals of moments capturing Blackfoot history. Indigenous people throughout North America knew him as a community leader, a powwow singer/dancer, a cultural advisor and a successful self-employed, self-taught, self-made entrepreneur. My family knew him as an amazing father, brother, uncle and grandfather.

To me, he was simply *"ninna"* (grandpa). He called me *"Omahksikimi"* (my Blackfoot name, given to me at birth) - it means *"big waters"*, always moving forward.

He died when I was 10 ...

... right up until the day he passed, he told me countless NAPI stories ... wherever we went ... as though he was somehow preparing me ...

You see, my *ninna* understood the limitless power of **traditional values**, and how seeking **integrity-based results** contributed directly to his tremendous career and life success. How we treat ourselves, how we treat our kids/family, how we treat our friends and how we treat our community is the true test of our Indigenous spirit and goodwill. Respect, humility, truth, wisdom, honesty, gratitude, love - they lay a foundation for everything else.

Without *sincere* traditional values, "culture" is just an act.

... or like my *ninna* would often say ... *"fancy facepaint, superb singing and a delightful drum don't always equal a good ndn"* ... very sad, but, true ...

So, who is this NAPI?

NAPI is a Blackfoot trickster ... a trouble maker ... a foolish being ... he teaches us what **not** to do. Blackfoot people have been using NAPI as an educational/motivational tool for thousands of years. Countless generations have survived, and thrived, from the priceless knowledge that NAPI introduces.

It is said that Napi could talk with all living things--the animals, plants, rocks, everything. He teased, pulled pranks, many times on himself. His actions began a cycle of existence. Every Blackfoot family has their own interpretation of the various Napi stories, but each has a common moral in the ending. One story might teach a lesson or prove a point; another story may tell of how a certain part of nature came to be. All Blackfoot people know of Napi, from the serious side of his creation to his foolish and spiteful deeds.

As a young boy, I gathered every NAPI story I could find (there's hundreds!). As a young man, I realized these valuable insights should be shared with the world. NAPI's powerful lessons of strength, struggle and traditional values are now yours.

Self improvement is a lifelong journey for us all, from children to Elders, from those taking their first steps towards a career to those in a leadership role. Whether young or old, employee or employer, our integrity and character define each of us. When you seek integrity-based results, it means you strive for success and excellence in ways that benefit everyone involved ... shared prosperity for all.

Sincere traditional values are a roadmap to career, life and relationship success. They're similar to social skills. School (and the workplace) is often the perfect training ground to hone your values. Everyday is a kaleidoscope, where many of the challenges we face in life (racism, sexism, colonialism, classism, egotism, capitalism, favoritism, nepotism, elitism, ageism, *gangster*-ism and just every other "-ism") are conveniently located, all under one roof - so take advantage of this unique situation and strengthen your values. The daily struggles you face are a test, the lifelong strengths you acquire are a validation.

As you absorb the NAPI series, consider these questions about yourself:

Do your values help you excel, or do they hold you back from your full potential? Do you seek integrity-based results?

To Your Prosperity,

Jason EagleSpeaker

NAPI

AND THE MICE

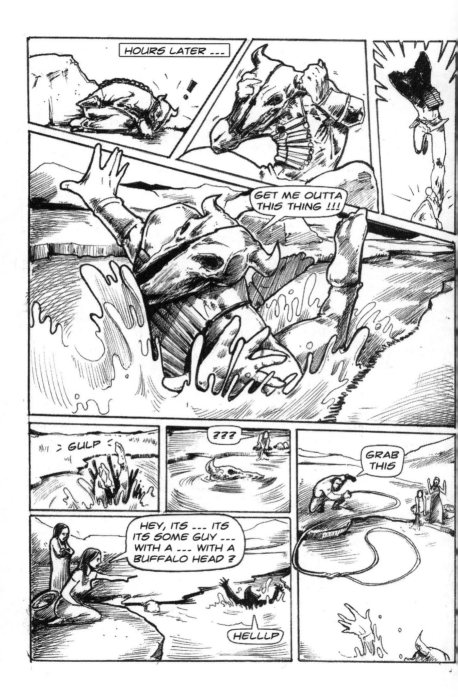

(*UNTIL THEN, BLACKFOOT PEOPLE HAD NEVER SEEN SOMEONE WITHOUT LONG HAIR)

LEARNING TO MAKE WISE CHOICES IS ALL PART OF GROWING UP. AT NINE YEARS OLD, I WAS STILL FIGURING OUT WHICH DECISIONS WERE WISE AND WHICH ONES WEREN'T. THE PATH TO FOLLOW WASN'T ALWAYS OBVIOUS. ONE DAY, A GROUP OF OLDER BOYS THAT I LOOKED UP TO TOLD ME TO "COME PARTY". THEY SURE DID MAKE IT SOUND FUN, SO I QUICKLY RAN HOME TO ASK MY GRANDPA (A WISE DECISION). OUT OF BREATH, I START TELLING MY GRANDPA ABOUT ALL THE FUN "PARTYING" AND HOW EXCITED I AM TO GO. AS IF ON CUE, GRANDPA STARTS TELLING ME THE STORY OF "NAPI AND THE MICE". IT TAUGHT ME TO THINK BEFORE I ACT, AND MAKE WISE CHOICES. WISDOM HELPED ME DECIDE WHICH PATHS TO FOLLOW.

"NAPI & THE MICE" TAUGHT ME WISDOM

HOW THE BLACKFOOT HARNESS WISDOM

Decisions, wise and unwise, have a rippling effect that can impact an entire community. The Blackfoot understand this and place high value on wisdom.

ELDERS - experience, knowledge and good judgment define Blackfoot Elders and their significant contribution to almost every aspect of our society.

FAMILY - culture-wise families are the primary ingredient in Blackfoot strength and success. Families that connect and share their wisdom always thrive.

CULTURAL - the wisest of the wise pass their teachings on to the next generation and keep our circle strong.

GOVERNANCE - making careful choices about who we elect, and trusting officials to also make wise decisions, is how the Blackfoot have governed for hundreds of years.

NATURE - the Blackfoot understand the wisdom nature provides and make it part of everyday life. Nature teaches many lessons.

COMMUNITY - our collective wisdom has kept Blackfoot communities strong and able to endure countless struggles.

HOW WISDOM CHANGED MY LIFE

"Think before doing, think before saying, think before writing" - my family said that to me many times. Simple, but, effective. I *still* say it to myself.

CHILD - praised for my positive choices, and corrected when I made negative ones, helped me understand the consequences of my actions.

TEEN - surrounded by intense peer pressure, it was tough finding a prosperous path. I focused on making productive choices.

ADULT - the decisions of youth can often have a huge impact on your adult life. Learn this to avoid undue hardship.

PARENT - wise decisions are not an option when you're responsible for others. Your actions impact others.

ENTREPRENEUR - successful entrepreneurs take calculated risks, think through all their decisions and pursue integrity-based results.

BUSINESS OWNER - as a business owner, you need to think strategically. Wisdom prepares you to target your most eager customers.

NAPI

AND THE GOPHERS

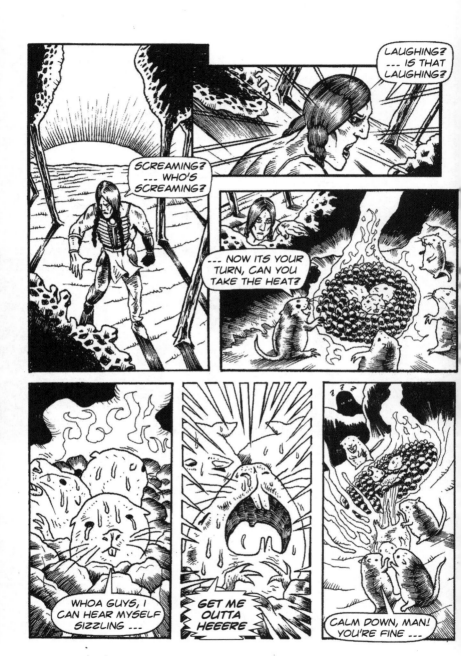

I FIRST HEARD "NAPI & THE GOPHERS" WHEN I ASKED MY GRANDPA ABOUT THIS KID THAT JOINED OUR POWWOW DANCE TROUPE. HE SURE WAS NICE GUY, BUT, SOME OF OUR POWWOW REGALIA STARTED GOING MISSING, MY FIRST LESSON IN THEFT. COMING FACE TO FACE WITH DISHONESTY IS CONFUSING, SO I SOUGHT OUT MY GRANDPA'S INSIGHT. "NAPI & THE GOPHERS" MADE ME REALIZE THAT DECEPTION CAN WEAR MANY MASKS AND THAT PAYING ATTENTION TO DETAIL IS OFTEN OUR ONLY REAL DEFENSE. IT GAVE ME THE COURAGE TO STAND UP TO ALL THE DISHONEST BEHAVIORS AND ENSURE ACCOUNTABILITY. LATER, WE FOUND OUT THAT THE NEW GUY HAD BEEN STEALING PRICELESS POWWOW REGALIA FOR YEARS AND WAS NOW TAKING OURS — DISHONESTY KNOWS NO LIMITS. I STILL THINK OF THIS NAPI STORY ANYTIME SOMEONE TRIES TO TAKE ADVANTAGE OF MY HONESTY.

"NAPI & THE GOPHERS" TAUGHT ME HONESTY

HOW THE BLACKFOOT HARNESS HONESTY

Without authenticity, there cannot be an honest relationship between people. The Blackfoot depend on the strength of honesty in many ways:

ELDERS - the importance of honesty shines through in all Elder teachings. Transferring traditional knowledge needs authenticity.

FAMILY - honesty about our strengths and struggles has made Blackfoot families a symbol of unity.

CULTURAL - expressing ourselves honestly is the foundation of our culture and has helped us to endure countless internal and external conflicts.

GOVERNANCE - transparency is what makes Blackfoot leadership a model for others to follow.

NATURE - the more we value the world around us, the better we interact with others. The Blackfoot understand this and it keeps us thriving against all odds.

COMMUNITY - Authenticity creates a strong vibrant community. Logic and reason are traits the Blackfoot rely on to ensure that all community members have input.

HOW HONESTY CHANGED MY LIFE

Honesty is a way of life that provides you with the best policy possible: when you are honest, you don't have to remember a lie. You can **always** be yourself. **Dishonesty takes much effort, honesty is effortless.**

CHILD - early on, I realized that honesty is appreciated by all. Dishonest behavior brings unwanted attention.

TEEN - choosing honesty and kindness as my guide has gave me the support and direction I needed, and the will to create my own path.

ADULT - honesty equals dependability, and that goes a long way in the adult world. As a dependable honest adult, opportunities soon surrounded me.

PARENT - honesty begins at home, and its up to parents to set the example.

ENTREPRENEUR - as an entrepreneur, trust and reliability are non-negotiable. Without them, potential clients will stay far away.

BUSINESS OWNER - your clients depend on you to be authentic. Protect your business, staff and customers against dishonest practices.

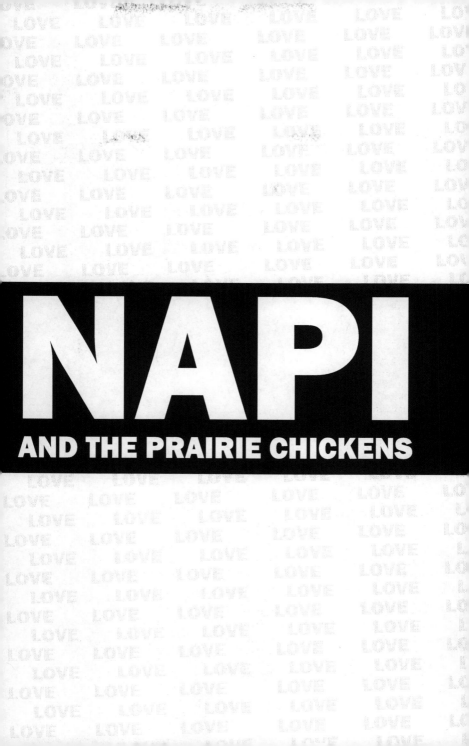

NAPI

AND THE PRAIRIE CHICKENS

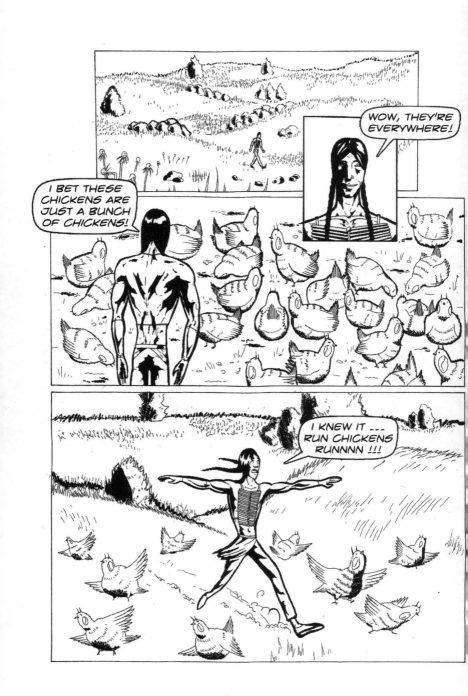

HOW'S THIS FOR MODESTY? AS A YOUNG BOY, I WAS QUITE THE CUTIE PIE. IN FACT, I WAS SO DARN CUTE OTHER BOYS THOUGHT I WAS A LI'L GIRL (MY BRAIDS, MAYBE?). ONE DAY I WAS KINDA JOKING AROUND WITH MY GRANDMA AND TOLD HER "I'M GONNA HAVE LOTSA GIRLFRIENDS". WITHOUT HESITATION MY GRANDMA TOLD ME THE STORY OF "NAPI AND THE PRAIRIE CHICKENS" ... AT FIRST I DIDN'T UNDERSTAND THE CONNECTION, AND WHAT IT HAD TO DO WITH MY DREAMS OF COUNTLESS LADY-FRIENDS, BUT, SOON IT ALL BECAME CLEAR — TREAT OTHERS WITH LOVE AND RESPECT, OR ELSE! AS A TEEN, I WATCHED MANY OF MY FRIENDS PURSUE QUANTITY OVER QUALITY — COLLECTING GIRLFRIENDS LIKE THEY'RE COLLECTING COMICS. "NAPI AND THE PRAIRIE CHICKENS" ALWAYS STUCK WITH ME, I TREAT EVERYONE AND EVERYTHING WITH LOVE, ESPECIALLY MYSELF, MY FAMILY AND MY BUSINESS.

"NAPI & THE PRAIRIE CHICKENS" TAUGHT ME LOVE

HOW THE BLACKFOOT HARNESS LOVE

There are endless kinds of love, and for the Blackfoot people, love has helped us thrive since the beginning of time:

ELDERS - there's nothing like the love of a grandparent. Blackfoot Elders are a valuable community resource and we provide them with lifelong care.

FAMILY - the power of family love has kept Blackfoot people united. Adversity has only brought us closer together.

CULTURAL - love for culture binds our communities. Love for ceremonies ensures their survival.

GOVERNANCE - our best community leaders build love into their work - promoting acceptance, decreased conflict and peace.

NATURE - love for nature takes very little effort, "all that casts a shadow is alive" is what my grandpa would say.

COMMUNITY - love for one another has helped Blackfoot people endure the most difficult of struggles. We always acknowledge each other, especially when afar and we always show love for our homelands.

HOW LOVE CHANGED MY LIFE

Assuming a loving, caring, protective role for my friends, my family and my business is an essential part of my success. Without love, my efforts would be hollow and limited.

CHILD - unconditional love is the foundation of all my successes.

TEEN - hormones raging, falling in/out of "love" - challenges any teen faces. Love is valuable, and confusing, best to tread lightly - steady those hormones.

ADULT - love for your career, love from your family, love in your relationships - who doesn't want that? Give love and get love. Let love be your default.

PARENT - the love you give your children must be without conditions - anything less and your children will grow up feeling the same.

ENTREPRENEUR - love for yourself and your ideas is a must, self doubt is the enemy of success. Love the fact you're self employed!

BUSINESS OWNER - create interesting and challenging work, create/follow a powerful mission statement. Empower your staff and success is inevitable.

NAPI

AND COYOTES JUMPING ON ICE

NINTENDO ENTERTAINMENT SYSTEM !!! MY NON-NDN FRIENDS AT SCHOOL HAD PILES OF GAME CARTRIDGES (YEP, THAT'S WHAT THEY WERE CALLED) - ALL THE GREATEST TITLES: CONTRA, SUPER MARIO 3, MEGA MAN, NINJA GAIDEN (OOH, AHH). I'D SIT BACK AND DROOL WATCHING EVERYONE TRADE/TALK GAMES AT RECESS. SO, HOW COME I WAS DROOLING ? ALTHOUGH I WAS LUCKY ENOUGH TO HAVE A NINTENDO AT HOME, I ONLY HAD TWO GAMES: DUCK HUNT AND MIKE TYSON'S PUNCHOUT ... WHICH EVERYONE HAD ALREADY. ONE DAY I ASKED MY GRANDMA TO BUY ANOTHER GAME. HER RESPONSE ??? THE STORY OF "NAPI & COYOTES JUMPING ON ICE". AN ATTITUDE OF GRATITUDE IS TRULY POWERFUL. HERE'S THE COOLEST PART: THERE WAS A MIKE TYSON'S PUNCHOUT GAME TOURNEY, WITH HUNDREDS OF COMPETITORS. I WON IT ALL AND RINGSIDE SEATS TO SEE MIKE TYSON FIGHT LIVE !!!

"NAPI & COYOTES JUMPING ON ICE" TAUGHT ME GRATITUDE

HOW THE BLACKFOOT HARNESS GRATITUDE

Appreciation and acknowledgment saturate every perspective of Blackfoot life. Imagine a world without gratitude - now that's scary!

ELDERS - living simply and efficiently has always been the way of Blackfoot Elders. They teach us to draw strength from our surroundings.

FAMILY - appreciating the "small" things has a major impact, Blackfoot families excel at this. Creating something from nothing is a strength.

CULTURAL - Blackfoot ceremonies and other cultural events rely very little on material items and fancy facilities.

GOVERNANCE - leadership is based on appreciation for Elders, Family, Culture, Nature and Community. Gratitude guides the most impactful decisions.

NATURE - grateful for all that nature provides can be seen in the everyday life of Blackfoot people.

COMMUNITY - although a tiny area compared to historical times, Blackfoot people still reside on their traditional lands. We have a community we can depend on for support.

HOW GRATITUDE CHANGED MY LIFE

I never tire of giving thanks. The more thankful I am, the better I feel. My life journey is an attitude of gratitude.

CHILD - giving children whatever they want can feel "good", but teaching them to value what they already have is much more rewarding.

TEEN - having the latest and greatest in material possessions seems hard to compete with, but, it's a never ending cycle. Appreciating what you have brings you a freedom that the shiniest objects never will.

ADULT - being grateful opens your eyes to the amazing opportunities that surround you.

PARENT - being responsible for raising a child is a joy that many never get the chance to experience. Be thankful.

ENTREPRENEUR - if you don't appreciate your own ideas, no one else will. *"Always Give Thanks!"*

BUSINESS OWNER - the success of your business depends on more than just you. Show appreciation to those you employ and those you service. Be a *"Grateful Guru"* and set the example.

NAPI

AND THE BULLBERRIES

GROWING UP ON THE BLOOD REZ, I WOULD ALWAYS HEAR PEOPLE SAY "BE HUMBLE" AND "HUMILITY IS A SACRED TEACHING". BEYOND THAT, I NEVER REALLY UNDERSTOOD EXACTLY WHAT HUMILITY WAS OR WHY IT'S IMPORTANT. AFTER SCHOOL ONE DAY, I TOLD MY GRANDPA ABOUT THIS KID WHO WAS ALWAYS BRAGGING ABOUT HIMSELF AND EVERYTHING HE OWNS AND EVERYTHING HE CAN DO AND THAT HIS WAY IS THE BEST WAY. AFTER A HEARTY LAUGH, MY GRANDPA TELLS ME THE STORY OF "NAPI & THE BULLBERRIES". WITHOUT THE HELP OF OTHERS, WE OFTEN OVERLOOK THE OBVIOUS ANSWERS. HUMILITY GRANTS ENORMOUS POWER TO ITS OWNER – COMPLETE FREEDOM FROM THE DESIRE TO IMPRESS, BE RIGHT, OR GET AHEAD OF OTHERS. A HUMBLE PERSON CONFIDENTLY RECEIVES OPPORTUNITY TO GROW AND IMPROVE. A TRULY HUMBLE LIFE RESULTS IN PATIENCE, FORGIVENESS, COMPASSION AND GUILT FREE INTEGRITY–BASED PROSPERITY ---

"NAPI & THE BULLBERRIES" TAUGHT ME HUMILITY

HOW THE BLACKFOOT HARNESS HUMILITY

Character has been described as who we are when you get to the core. Who you are affects what you do. Humility is how you see yourself.

ELDERS - humility is best learned by example, Elders are that humble beacon that we all aspire to emulate.

FAMILY - thinking of others first keeps our family ties strong - humility, not ego, ensures powerful bonds.

CULTURAL - personal accomplishments rarely go unrecognized, our cultural events always take the time to honor.

GOVERNANCE - admitting and learning from mistakes makes leaders more approachable, more honest, and connects them to the people they lead. This is the Blackfoot way.

NATURE - underestimating the forces of nature is not a wise move, the Blackfoot understand this and aspire to achieve harmony with our surroundings.

COMMUNITY - Recognizing our own strengths and struggles keeps our communities moving forward in ways that benefit all. Opportunities that engage and evolve keep us strong.

HOW HUMILITY CHANGED MY LIFE

It's common to see ambition and humility as opposites. They are not. They're **comfortable partners**. Humility makes ambition unselfish and powerful

CHILD - from the beginning, we all learn how to respond, how to apologize, how to be grateful and how to serve our community.

TEEN - making sure teenagers understand where their real value comes from, that's the challenge we all face as parents - embrace it.

ADULT - giving thanks keeps us humble uniting our gifts, abilities and desire to succeed strengthens our efforts.

PARENT - from the very beginning humility must be consistently modeled as a lifestyle, not an on-again, off-again example. Follow a humble path.

ENTREPRENEUR - humility is the missing ingredient to your success. It makes you confident without conceit; supportive without being submissive.

BUSINESS OWNER - humility listens, humility tests, humility admits. True leaders harness humility and inspire by being a living example.

NAPI
AND THE ELK

EVER HEARD OF HUFFING? HOW 'BOUT GLUE SNIFFING? PILL POPPING? BLACKING OUT? ... AS A YOUNG KID, I HAD HEARD OF THEM ALL, BUT, WE WERE TOO BUSY HAVING KID FUN. AS A TEEN, I STARTED SEEING LOTS OF MY FRIENDS LOOKING TO GET HIGH ON MORE THAN JUST LIFE. AS MORE AND MORE OF MY FRIENDS CHOSE ADDICTIONS, I BEGAN TELLING MYSELF "GEEZ, MY FRIENDS LOOK LIKE THEY'RE HAVING THE TIME OF THEIR LIVES, MAYBE I SHOULD GIVE THIS ADDICTION STUFF A TRY". LIKE ANYTHING, I DECIDED TO ASK MY GRANDMA ABOUT IT (MY GRANDPA HAD PASSED ON). SHE TOLD ME THE STORY OF "NAPI & THE ELK". IT TOOK ME AWHILE TO MAKE THE CONNECTION, BUT, THEN IT HIT ME — BLIND TRUST. FOLLOWING OTHERS EXAMPLE CAN HAVE BOTH GOOD AND BAD OUTCOMES — IT'S UP TO EACH OF US TO FIGURE OUT THE BEST EXAMPLES TO FOLLOW AND THE ONES WE SHOULD SIMPLY IGNORE ...

"NAPI & THE ELK" TAUGHT ME TRUST

HOW THE BLACKFOOT HARNESS TRUST

Trust is an important part of every aspect of Blackfoot life, in all we do and in the way we conduct ourselves.

ELDERS - truth is the basis of leading an honorable life. Our Elders teach us this by their example. Whatever they tell us, we pay close attention, trying not to make mistakes when we listen.

FAMILY - we revere our family bonds and the trust we have in one another. Families that thrive are built on trust.

CULTURAL - trust is how we come to the still quiet place of our ancestors. Trust is the root of Blackfoot culture - trusting ceremony, trusting protocol.

GOVERNANCE - close daily contact with community members ensures those who govern us are held to a high standard.

NATURE - trusting in nature to provide has kept the Blackfoot strong since the beginning of time. Today, that trust keeps us connected to our surroundings.

COMMUNITY - the strongest communities are built on trust, and working together to raise our children ensures their resilience.

HOW TRUST CHANGED MY LIFE

A strong foundation of any relationship is built on trust. Without trust, life becomes lonely. Trust allows us to have meaningful relationships with others.

CHILD - if trust is important in a family, children will value it to. Model trust.

TEEN - as a teenager, figuring out who to trust can be tough. Trustworthy friends and mentors are a must.

ADULT - as precious as trust is, it can easily be lost. Be that person others can depend on. Once trust is gone, it's difficult to earn back.

PARENT - imagine that your children don't trust you, feels gross doesn't it? That vision alone demonstrates how important it is.

ENTREPRENEUR - trust in yourself, trust in your ideas and trust in your product - your success depends on it.

BUSINESS OWNER - trust is modelled, and it goes both ways, between the boss and their team. Trust your staff to do the work you hired them for, and they will trust you to lead them into a fruitful future.

NAPI
AND THE ROCK

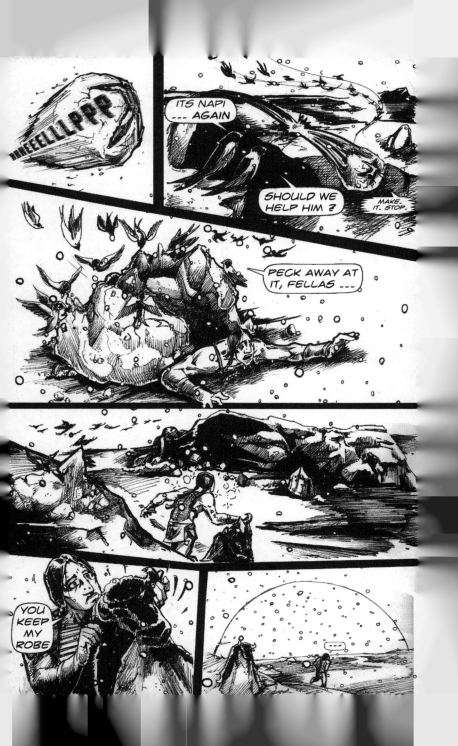

I FIRST HEARD "NAPI & THE ROCK" AFTER MY GRANDPA DISCOVERED MY PLANS TO TAKE BACK A BIKE THAT I HAD GIFTED TO ONE OF MY FRIENDS. I DECIDED I WANTED TO KEEP IT FOR MYSELF INSTEAD --- JUST AS I WAS ABOUT TO LEAVE TO GET IT BACK, MY GRANDPA TOLD ME THIS NAPI STORY. I QUICKLY LISTENED AND LEFT. STARING AT 'MY' BIKE IN MY FRIEND'S YARD, ALL THE LESSONS OF THIS STORY SUDDENLY BEGAN SURGING THROUGHOUT MY BODY. I HAD WHAT GROWNUPS CALL 'AN EPIPHANY' --- I FELT THE TRUE POWER OF RESPECT --- RESPECT FOR MYSELF AND MY DECISIONS, RESPECT FOR MY FRIENDS AND THEIR OWN DESIRES, AND RESPECT FOR ELDERS AND THE WISDOM THEY PROVIDE. NAPI CHANGED IT ALL.

"NAPI & THE ROCK" TAUGHT ME RESPECT

HOW THE BLACKFOOT HARNESS RESPECT

Historically, respect played a major role in all decisions, especially those that would impact our entire community.

ELDERS - respecting Elders is a universal Blackfoot trait. To us, they're the knowledge keepers that possess the key to enduring enlightenment.

FAMILY - respecting family and our unique perspectives has kept us strong for countless generations.

CULTURAL - respecting protocols gives us a deep appreciation for patience and diligence.

GOVERNANCE - respecting the democratic process gives us the power to choose those who truly represent our needs and interests.

NATURE - respecting the Earth strengthens our connections and gives us a vision for living in harmony with our surroundings.

COMMUNITY - respect keeps us united and creates a deep sense of comradery. Although our communities are rural and often isolated, connecting with other tribes/families through cultural events (like powwows, round dances etc) is universally important.

HOW RESPECT CHANGED MY LIFE

Respect led directly to my success. It opened doors for me that took my relationships, my career and my well-being to a whole new level.

CHILD - respecting the wisdom of my Elders allowed all those "teachable moments" to really shine through. Valuable knowledge I gained as a child still guides me as an adult.

TEEN - respecting authority made all the difference in my academics. It helped me to believe I can achieve.

ADULT - respecting my family, my community and my colleagues has given me the support I need to succeed. I emulate the great.

PARENT - respecting my children starts with self-respect. Respecting their point of view builds trust and confidence.

ENTREPRENEUR - respecting my talents for knowledge sharing and true self expression provides me with the determination to excel, and thrive.

BUSINESS OWNER - clients respect expertise, that alone propels me to improve, innovate and diversify our services. Respect equals loyalty. Loyalty builds a successful business.

12 Powerful Ways Respect Can Lead You To Success

RESPECT

There is no greater honor than the respect of your children, your family, your peers, and your community. There is much power in respect - *the simple act of treating others as though they matter*. The rewards of being respected and giving respect to others are beyond measure. Sincere respect is essential for success and a necessary step towards *integrity-based* results. The fantastic thing about respect is that, with minimal effort you can achieve maximum impact. In school, respecting your education can lead to scholarships and academic accolades. In the workplace, respecting your colleagues creates unity and builds lifelong connections. At home, respecting points of view allows for open communication and bonding.

As an employee, respect is the cornerstone of customer service. Easily earn respect by *listening closely* to what others are saying and *thinking calmly* about your response.

As an employer, respect is vital to team success. Master your emotions and strive to build strong relationships, you will reap the benefits of respectfulness and real happiness.

As an entrepreneur, respect allows you to: fully appreciate your efforts, relate effectively to your clients, and motivate others. Respect stems from pride, hope, and enthusiasm, it frees entrepreneurs from the obstacles of low self-esteem, hopelessness, and anger. Respect builds valuable bridges.

As a business owner, earning the respect of customers and contacts is imperative. Constantly improving your services, diversifying your talent pool, and proactively responding to feedback will earn the respect/loyalty you need to succeed.

In ourselves, it begins with self-respect. The view we have of ourselves affects not only our attitudes and behaviors but also our views of other people. Offer yourself unconditional respect - courage and gratitude will grow organically.

In relationships, respect is a foundation. We all have our own point of view, but, it's important to think *empathically*. True respect is seeing someone, flaws and all, and yet still feeling appreciation for their unique talents and insights.

In parenting, mutual respect is a must. Children learn *most* from the example *you* set for them, respecting each other as parents is a priority. Chaos and calm are equally contagious.

In families, respect is crucial, but, complicated. Whether you live together or see each other just once a year, it can sometimes take a special kind of respect to keep your cool. I call it the *"Respect Perspective"* - always value your family, because many people out there have no family at all.

As kids, understanding the importance of respect is critical, so they can communicate effectively with others throughout their lives. *Teaching* respect is as easy as *showing* respect.

As a teenager, respect can often be a struggle to maintain. The value of upholding respect increases your chances of success and relating better with people in your everyday life.

As an adult, respect is a necessity. A thriving relationship, a successful career and academic excellence - all are based in respect, for yourself, your kids/family and your community. The simplest way to be respectful is to *not* be disrespectful.

As a role model, self-respect is a prerequisite. Turning your struggles into strengths is motivational, and how you treat others on your path to success is inspirational. Model strong moral values and your impact will be felt for generations.

RESPECT
... *seek* it
... *adapt* it
... *model* it
... *praise* it

RESPECT PERSPECTIVE
HOW TO HARNESS THE IMMENSE POWER OF RESPECT

CLASSROOM ACTIVITIES:

In groups of 3-5 students, identify a school problem caused by a lack of respect. Research the causes of the problem, the extent of the problem and the impact of the problem. How many people does this problem affect? How are people affected? Does this problem cost the school money each year? Why should people care about this problem? Brainstorm possible solutions to the problem. Who can solve this problem? What can students do to aid in this solution? Evaluate the alternatives. Is there a solution that can be implemented?

Have students write a letter to someone they respect and admire. Letters should reference why they respect this person, the impact this person has had on them, and the way in which the student would like to honor this person (if they could). Create a *"How To Respect"* educational display or pamphlet for use at schools, with younger children or even the community. Have children create a *"We Respect Differences"* collage, from old magazines.

IN THE WORKPLACE:

When you make an uncomfortable judgment, instead of burying it, see it as an opportunity to develop, learn, and grow. Accept accountability, ask for understanding and move forward.

Clearly defined expectations and boundaries helps create a culture of respect and holds everyone accountable (have employees help draft the code of standards and expectations).

Changing a culture of disrespect is a system wide objective - which starts at the top. *What the leader expects the leader has to model.* Leadership must also be held accountable.

What you praise, you perpetuate. Lift up the positives of respect, honor, civility, and diversity. These are the strengths of your organization and the virtues that make it great.

Create an inclusive work environment. Only by recognizing and respecting individual differences and qualities can your organization fully realize its potential.

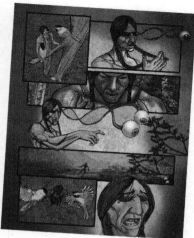

NAPI
The Trixster, Vol 2
... the lessons continue
(COMING SOON)

ABOUT THE AUTHOR

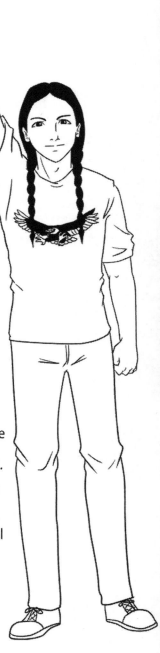

Only a few short years after the *Occupation of Alcatraz*, the *Wounded Knee Incident* and the *Shootout at Pine Ridge Reservation*, a boy was conceived.

Born in Seattle, raised on four reservations and in two cities, **Jason EagleSpeaker** is both Blackfoot and Duwamish – the one his family called *"that li'l half-buffalo, half-salmon ndn"*.

Today, he is a nationally published education author, graphic novelist, successful social entrepreneur and grassroots communications consultant. Based in Calgary, Canada, he travels extensively with his family, creating endless non-fiction works. His hard hitting true stories focus on revealing the modern experiences of Indigenous people (the strengths *and* the struggles).

Be sure to order his book, *"UNeducation: A Residential School Graphic Novel"* - the chilling chronicles of a family's exploitation in the mandatory residential school/boarding school system.

You can connect with Jason online at **www.eaglespeaker.com**, or just follow him on Facebook.

Made in the USA
Columbia, SC
14 February 2018